WHY BOTHER WITH TRUTH?

Arriving at Knowledge in a Skeptical Society

James Beilby

teaches as an adjunct professor at Bethel College and Seminary in St. Paul, MN. He also holds a research position at Bethel Theological Seminary. He is completing his Ph.D. at Marquette University in philosophy and theology and is currently writing his dissertation on the topic of religious epistemology. James received his M.A. from Bethel Theological Seminary in 1994, and his B.A. from Northwestern College (St. Paul, MN) in 1991. He has published numerous articles in scholarly journals including *Faith and Philosophy, Religious Studies, International Journal for Philosophy of Religion,* and *Philosophia Christi.* In addition to his dissertation, he is working on a number of books, including an edited volume forthcoming from InterVarsity Press on the problem of divine foreknowledge and freedom.

James makes his home in Blaine, Minnesota with his wife, Michelle, and their daughters, Sierra and Madeline. Michelle is a youth pastor at Brookdale Covenant Church in Minneapolis, Minnesota.

Besides his academic interests, James enjoys playing golf, basketball, and football. He also thoroughly enjoys the distinction of being one of a very small group of “theol

David K. Clark

has his Ph.D. in Philosophy from Northwestern University and his M.A. from Trinity Evangelical Divinity School. He teaches theology and Christian thought at Bethel Theological Seminary in St. Paul, Minnesota. He is Dean of Bethel's Center for Biblical and Theological Foundations.

Besides having written many journal articles, he has written such books as *The Pantheism of Alan Watts* (InterVarsity Press) and *Dialogical Apologetics* (Baker), He is co-editor of *Readings in Christian Ethics: Theory and Method* and *Readings in Christian Ethics: Issues and Applications* (Baker).

David was born and lived for fifteen years in Tokyo, Japan. For ten years, the Clark family lived in Toccoa, Georgia, where David and Sandy both taught at Toccoa Falls College. David moved with his family to New Brighton, Minnesota, in 1988 to teach at Bethel. Sandy, his wife, is a development officer for Bethel College and Seminary and writes freelance on family life issues. David and Sandy have two soccer-playing sons: Tyler (18) and Ryan (14).

INTRODUCTION

Truth would be mighty useful to have. Too bad it seems so elusive. So why even bother with truth? People have struggled with the idea of truth for millennia. The great Greek philosopher, Socrates (470-399 B.C.), died by drinking hemlock poison, the death penalty of the day. The Senate convicted him of worshiping different gods and corrupting Athenian youth. Socrates constantly irritated his countrymen by pressing annoying questions. But his real purpose was to find truth. Socrates held that "the unexamined life is not worth living." So he pursued the truth about the unchanging moral principles that lead to the good life.

Sophists, contemporaries of Socrates, came to Athens from other lands. They challenged the patterns of Greek life. Did the moral precepts of Athens stand on natural (and therefore lasting) principles? Or did Athens guide its life by humanly created (and therefore changeable) custom? One Sophist, Gorgias, claimed that nothing exists; or if it does, it can't be understood; or if it can, it can't be expressed. The Sophists declared that no one will find any ultimate truth.

Western intellectual history has generally sided with Socrates. The development of theology, science, and philosophy attests to the value people place on truth. Yet, in our "enlightened" times, Sophist-like viewpoints abound. They're part of the nip in the cultural air. Many people now doubt the human ability to find truth; an attitude of suspicion and skepticism is now more often the rule rather than the exception. People seem to hold out about as much hope of finding truth as they do of taking a flight to Never Never Land with Peter Pan. In other words, many people today ask the so-called *Skeptical Question*: Since we disagree about so many things, do we *really* know what we *think* we know?

The Skeptical Question is difficult. With such questions, it seems that the more we think about them, the more complex they get. It's one step forward, five steps back. We all face questions with deep theological and philosophical implications, but these issues seem more manageable when they come up in real-life situations. So let me make the question more concrete. Here's a real life situation that raises the Skeptical Question in several different ways.

Mary is a middle-aged mother who recently became a Christian. She grew up in a home that was profoundly hostile to the Christian faith. Her parents taught her that God doesn't exist, and, what is more, that those who think that God *does* exist are uninformed and ignorant. As she grew up, Mary never questioned this belief. Indeed, especially in college, her skepticism deepened. Her philosophy professor at the university taught that Immanuel Kant had decisively refuted all the arguments for God's existence. Her religious studies teacher asserted that none of the religiously significant events recorded in the Bible really happened. And her psychology instructor taught that Sigmund Freud had explained (and explained away) all religious belief as being merely the product of "wish-fulfillment." That is, according to Freud, we want the security of believing in a loving God; so we try to get ourselves to think that God does exist. Mary knew that there were other professors who disagreed with these ideas, but she never really understood why.

After college Mary got married, had a son, and got divorced, but she never questioned the basic atheism of her parents. Then she moved into a new neighborhood and made some new friends, several of whom were Christians! Her new friends surprised her. For one thing, they seemed normal. They talked about all the same things her other friends talked about: movies, politics, raising teenagers, and so on. They didn't talk *just* about religion—although occasionally, to Mary's discomfort, the subject did come up. Mary was also surprised to learn that they seemed very bright, in fact, every bit as intelligent as Mary herself. They seemed aware of the objections to belief in God that Mary had learned about in college, but they didn't find them compelling. Through these friendships, Mary found herself accepting an invitation to attend church, and after two years of regular attendance—a period characterized by deep thought and soul-searching—she became a Christian.

As happy as Mary was that she had taken this step of commitment, however, she was truly worried about how her family would respond. In fact, it was largely this fear that kept her from becoming a Christian sooner. Mary knew that her father would disapprove, and she expected that her son, now a sophomore philosophy major in college, might find her commitment offensive. But she finally decided she had to share this with her family, and so she invited them both over one afternoon to break the news. The result was predictable but still very upsetting. As she expected, her father, Peter, argued that the whole idea of God's existence is intellectually naive. Peter launched into a speech about his long-held belief that the lack of evidence for Christian belief requires us to withhold belief in God. God's existence can't be proved; in fact, it can be explained away. After all, science proves that the whole idea of God is unnecessary. So intelligent people should reject God's existence!

Mary's son, Paul, as she expected, also thought she made a mistake. But his reasoning differed from his grandfather's. Given what he was learning at the university, Paul argued that the whole idea of believing that it's *true* (for all people in all places) that the Christian God exists (and other gods do not) is philosophically naive and intellectually arrogant! But to Mary's surprise, Paul argued that his grandfather's emphasis on the proof or disproof of God's existence is equally naive. To his mind, both Mary and Peter are wrong to assume that there's anything like "objective truth," an idea he finds absurd. Instead, Paul thinks that religions and beliefs about God are simply ways of coping with reality. Some people need something like religion to help them through life. He does not.

This conversation left Mary deeply confused and disturbed. Her father and son posed powerful objections to her belief, objections that were similar in some respects, but very different in others. Both Peter and Paul raised the Skeptical Question, but did so in very different ways.

How could Mary answer these skeptical challenges? Before trying to answer that question, it's best to understand the question—in both its varieties—a little better. The Skeptical Question comes in both modern and postmodern varieties, and both of these have an important history.

THE SHAPE OF *MODERN* SKEPTICISM:

No Knowledge Without Evidence

Chapter 1

If the ancient and medieval worlds largely agreed with Socrates, it seems the contemporary world increasingly sides with the Sophists. Today people think that we must explain our reasons for thinking that truth really exists—especially a single religious truth. How did the Skeptical Question become so influential? Let's look first at how it arose and took shape in its *modern* form.

As the modern era dawned, a French philosopher named René Descartes ("day-**cart**") (1596-1650) began thinking about knowledge in new ways. Like Socrates, Descartes believed fervently that we can find the truth. He feared *skepticism*, the doctrine that all knowledge claims are suspect or unsupportable, and he hoped that certitude in knowledge could overcome skepticism. By focusing on skepticism, Descartes turned the attention of modern philosophers to *epistemology*, to the study of theories of knowledge.

In order to avoid skepticism, Descartes decided to set very high standards for what he would count as *knowledge*. If the standards of knowledge are very high, and if our knowledge claims meet those standards, then (Descartes reasoned) we can surely avoid skepticism. So he posed his problem this way: Either we achieve absolute *certitude* (and genuine knowledge) or we give in to *skepticism* (and admit ignorance). This way of thinking—that we must either achieve certainty or else admit defeat—profoundly shaped the modern mentality.

Impressed by early developments in science and

mathematics, Descartes made a new beginning in his search for absolutely certain knowledge. Since the senses can mislead us, Descartes distrusted them. Instead, he chose to build human knowledge on reason alone. This is the method called *rationalism*.[1] Like mathematics, and especially geometry, rationalism begins with absolutely certain starting points and carefully moves to absolutely certain conclusions. Descartes adapted this geometry-like, rationalist method to all fields of knowledge.

To answer skepticism decisively, Descartes decided he would accept only absolutely undoubtable beliefs. So he set for himself a very high standard, the severest test possible. He proposed a thought experiment, a "worst possible case" scenario. If, in the worst of all possible situations, Descartes' method could produce certain knowledge, then he reasoned he could take it as a decisive answer to skepticism. So here's Descartes' test: What happens if I assume that a powerful demon is deceiving me at every moment? Do I still have knowledge?

Descartes thought so. "Even if a terrible demon did his level best to deceive me," Descartes thought to himself, "there is still one thing I know: I'm being deceived. Thus, I'm thinking. And therefore, I exist." This is Descartes' famous conclusion: "I think; therefore, I am." In the worst possible situation for discovering knowledge, Descartes thought he could achieve certitude. And from this slender platform, he thought he could extend his knowledge to include knowledge of God and of the external world. Skepticism is answered—or so Descartes thought.

Descartes' ideas hit two snags. First, Descartes' supposedly infallible method failed to achieve undoubtable results. In fact, it produced contradictions! Two other thinkers, Baruch Spinoza (1632-1677) and Gottfried Leibniz (1646-1716), followed his supposedly airtight method, but arrived at different conclusions. The three philosophers produced three theories about the nature of reality (i.e., three views on metaphysics) that canceled each other out!

This contradiction demolished Descartes' claim that the geometric method defeats skepticism by producing undoubtable knowledge.

Second, things got worse when mathematicians discovered *competing* geometries! Suppose we draw a line *l* and a point *p* in a flat plane. Usually we think that there's only one line which is parallel to line *l* and passes through point *p*. The ancient Greek mathematician, Euclid, assumed just that. But Georg Riemann (1826-1866) wondered what would happen if he presupposed that *no lines*, parallel to *l*, pass through *p*. (This happens if you think of curved space rather than flat planes.) And Nikolai Lobatchevsky (1793-1856) assumed that an *infinite number of lines*, parallel to *l*, pass through *p*. Here's the surprise: Riemann and Lobatchevsky developed geometries that are just as logical and consistent as Euclid's! Thus, even geometry itself led, not to certitude, but to contradictory conclusions, *depending on the starting assumptions*.

Though the rationalism of Descartes fizzled, the modern world produced another response to the Skeptical Question. Francis Bacon (1561-1626) made an early attempt to understand scientific method. Bacon wasn't really a scientist in the modern sense. (For example, he had no idea of testing a hypothesis.) Instead he relied heavily on observation. He began with the five senses and then extracted generalizations directly from those observations by cataloguing, comparing, and distinguishing whatever he studied. Bacon's approach to science starts with the senses, and this is the heart of an epistemology that is the opposite of rationalism. It's called *empiricism*.

Many people think that trusting the senses is an obvious thing to do. But surprisingly the empirical tradition also led to skepticism. For example, David Hume's (1711-1776) philosophy led him to skepticism when he followed his epistemology rigorously. Hume said that knowledge is rooted in experience. If we want absolute certitude, we must limit our beliefs to what we can *actually experience*. Hume's famous discussion of *causation* illustrates his point. I can actually experience a cue ball rolling, hear it striking the 10 ball, and see it rolling away at an angle. I might conclude that the cue ball *caused* the 10 ball to move. But sticking strictly to what I directly experience through my senses, I don't actually experience the causation. I only actually experience isolated events—balls rolling, touching, and making sounds.

We do observe isolated events regularly happening next to each other. Two events—the sun's rising and the rooster's crowing—routinely occur together. But we observe no direct relation, no essential connection, between the isolated events. So Hume's rules of epistemology, rigorously followed, lead us to a skepticism in the face of disjointed facts. We may experience bits of information, but we can't ever know the patterns, relationships, or connections between the facts. Thus, present facts have no relation to future facts, and one case has no logical connection to similar cases. So if I repeatedly see the sun rising and setting, this doesn't *prove* that it will do so tomorrow, even though common sense leads me to presume that it will. We may achieve data, but never knowledge and certainly not wisdom. In fact, Hume argued that we can't even prove that the world around us exists! So Hume's empiricism led to skepticism just as rationalism did.

As these two philosophical traditions (rationalism and empiricism) ground down toward a negative result, science was enjoying smashing success. A large boost came with the incredible work of Isaac Newton (1642-1727). His work was so renowned that Alexander Pope proclaimed,

> Nature and Nature's laws lay hid in night:
> God said, *Let Newton be!* and all was light.

Newton reflected on the method he used to make his astonishing scientific advances. His theory of knowledge was neither the overly rational ideal of Descartes nor the purely empirical method of Hume.

The main line of scientific advance moved, rather, by using a method that pulls together rationalism (the ideas of the mind) with empiricism (the observations of the senses).

Newton's life overlapped with the beginning of a Golden Age called the Enlightenment. The Enlightenment era (roughly the 1700s) was an important high point of modernism. Many intellectuals—people of literature, science, and philosophy—shared a central Enlightenment goal. They valued human happiness and the liberty gained through social progress guided by human reason. Their dream required shaking off the social influence of religious traditions and superstitions from the past, for they believed that religion often leads to war. They believed a new, brilliant era lay ahead. The future held promise for a new, harmonious culture directed by human reason. Gradually, as science leaped from one success to another, modern people came to see science as the primary form through which human reason would solve social dilemmas and create a bright future.

By the late nineteenth century, the dominant intellectual ethos of Western culture came to be that science *alone* is the legitimate cultural authority and the prime example of rationality. Modern thinkers came to see science as the specific form of reason that would produce the social progress they desired. This singular stress on the supremacy of science had broad implications. For one thing, people in other walks of life felt the need to meet the standard of proof specified by the scientific ideal. In the early twentieth century, a group of philosophers and scientists known as logical positivists argued explicitly that all language should meet the standards of empirical science. The ideas of the *logical positivists* gained enormous influence in the early and middle portion of this century, especially in the academic world, where their ideas affected (and infected) many other disciplines.

The logical positivists had far-ranging goals. They sought to develop a system by which they could prove every belief. *Logic* provided the means to be *positive* about beliefs—hence the name. They left nothing to chance or supposition. Since beliefs must be expressed by means of words and sentences, they focused on language. They tried to specify a method which would show what words mean, a method by which they could be *sure* that words have those (and only those) meanings. So they developed a criterion by which they could determine which words are meaningful (have a properly established meaning), and which words are meaningless (don't have a properly established meaning). This criterion, called the *Verification Criterion of Meaning*, specifies that for a word or sentence to be meaningful, it must be verifiable by the five senses (empirically).[2] The word *tree* is verifiable and thus meaningful since we can see, feel, and even smell trees. But the word *God* and sentences like "God loves me" aren't empirically verifiable, and therefore don't even get to be called *false*. Rather, like the sentence, "Yellow circles weigh 117 pounds," they're just meaningless!

Taken together, the emphases on science as the ideal path to knowledge and on empirical observation as the proper means to determine the meaning of words together reinforce a particular theory of what is required for knowledge. For a belief to be *knowledge*, according to this theory, it must be supported by adequate evidence. This emphasis on adequate evidence expresses a philosophical doctrine called evidentialism. According to *evidentialism*, every human being has a duty to believe *only* those claims that are supported by sufficient evidence. It's not just irrational, but it's actually *immoral* to believe anything without sufficient evidence. Evidentialism wasn't a new doctrine; it had been around for a hundred years or more. But the prominence of science reinforced evidentialism.

Notice how easily the emphasis on science fits with the requirements of evidentialism and positivism. Evidentialism demands positive evidence for every belief. Positivism asserts that meaningful assertions are found only through empirical verification. Only science (or something very much like it) produces knowledge that meets these requirements. Thus, the strong emphasis on science fits very well with evidentialism and positivism: If a belief doesn't fit in with well-established scientific beliefs or isn't the sort of belief that is discovered through normal scientific practices, then it isn't rational or it doesn't count as genuine knowledge. And again, this means every person *ought* to be agnostic about religious claims.

Several theses, taken together, aptly summarize the Skeptical Question in its modern form.

> *Evidentialism*: Every belief must be supported by adequate evidence. In fact, believing something without adequate evidence is *immoral*! Of course, many people think that religious beliefs never achieve sufficient evidence. And if this is so, then, given the requirements of evidentialism, religious convictions are never justified and should not be believed.
>
> *Positivism*: Only assertions that are verifiable by the senses are meaningful. Empirical and scientific facts are intellectually meaningful, but values or religious assertions never are. Therefore, according to positivism, the content of religious beliefs is no more meaningful than a sneeze.
>
> *Scientism*: Everyone agrees that science produces well-supported beliefs. But scientism goes beyond this. According to scient*ism*, science *alone* produces rational beliefs. At a minimum, weak scientism says that science is more rational, more valuable, or more important than non-science.

In the modernist mentality, verification by

empirical evidence, sensory data, or scientific facts is the standard, the high-jump crossbar that any knowledge claim must leap over. Modern skeptics hold that religious beliefs never clear this very high crossbar. Thus, religious convictions never count as genuine knowledge. So the Skeptical Question *in its modern form* goes something like this: "Do we *really* know what we *think* we know—especially in religion—when our beliefs are not properly based on empirical evidence?" For religious belief, the implication is plain: Unless we can give strong proof for God's existence, then evidentialism and empiricism require us to disbelieve. If the evidence is less than compelling, it's wrong—irrational and even immoral—to believe in God. A modern skeptic like Peter (from the case study) would sum up his view of religion in this way: Unless believers can give scientific evidence for their private, religious ideas, they really shouldn't believe in God.

THE SHAPE OF *POSTMODERN* SKEPTICISM:

No Knowledge, Only Perspectives

Chapter 2

Like those who lived in the modern age, many people today take a skeptical stance toward religion. Yet a new movement called *postmodernism* has pushed beyond modern skepticism. Postmodernism is a teeming jungle of attitudes and ideas. At its core, postmodernism sees modernity—especially the Enlightenment—as wrong-headed. Modernism stresses rationalism, absolutism, and positivism. According to Enlightenment gospel, the individual—liberated from religious authority and appealing to reason—can discover truth and reach happiness. But postmodernism has a strong allergic reaction to these ideals.

The important taproots of postmodern philosophy are embedded in the modern era. A helpful starting point is the great modern German philosopher, Immanuel Kant (1724-1804). Early on, Kant followed the rationalism of Gottfried Leibniz. Though he was a meticulously-minded bachelor who never traveled beyond his small hometown of Königsberg in eastern Prussia, he read widely. And after poring over David Hume, Kant awoke from a "dogmatic slumber." As a result he abandoned Leibnizian philosophy—he called it "rotten dogmatism"—and set about to create a new and different epistemology in response to Hume's challenge. This new critical epistemology became Kant's answer to the Skeptical Question.

Kant made a decisive shift: Rather than putting the emphasis on just the senses or only the mind, he argued that *both the senses and the mind* contribute to human knowledge. Like Newton, Kant used both rational and empirical themes, but he did so in a rather different way. Kant argued that knowledge arises as the data of the senses are interpreted by the categories of the mind. Kant agreed with Hume that knowledge *begins* in experience. But unlike Hume, he said there's also a kind of knowledge that isn't *based on* experience. This second kind of knowledge, arising in the mind and not from the senses, produces what Hume never found—the connections or relations between the facts.

Remember what Hume said about *causation*: It's impossible to know that one event causes another. Facts always remain disconnected data points, and so we never get beyond random information. But Kant argued that the principle of causation is a category that's innate to the mind. Causality isn't observed directly. It's hard-wired into the mind. So the mind acts like a new computer with a pre-loaded word-processing program. The computer has no actual documents—no letters, articles, or term papers—stored on its hard disk. But a structure, a program, for receiving files is loaded when it's built. Similarly, the mind is pre-wired with empty categories like the principle of causality. These categories contain no actual information about the world. Prior to experience, we can know in *general* that causes produce effects, but we don't know about any *particular* cause-effect relation. In sum, the categories in the mind stand ready to receive and structure the facts of experience, and experience fills the categories with content. Both elements work together to produce knowledge.

This synthesis brilliantly answered Hume's challenge, but it carried the seeds of a new kind of skepticism. Kant's critical philosophy has been likened to the Copernican Revolution. When Copernicus proposed that the sun is at the center of our solar system, he completely reoriented astronomy. Similarly, Kant completely reoriented epistemology. People generally assumed that the *world shapes the contents of the mind*, but Kant said that in theoretical reason, *the structure of the mind shapes our view of the world.*

Reality no longer "simply" structures knowledge in the mind; the mind constructs knowledge of reality. This intellectual Copernican Revolution was as massive a reversal as putting the sun in place of the earth at the center of the solar system. Its implications would be momentous.

What did Kant's philosophy mean for human knowledge? Kant asserted that *theoretical* reason allows access only to *reality as it appears to us.* Theoretical reason can't reach *reality as it is.* This seems to concede skepticism. But Kant believed that what he called *practical* reason (as opposed to *theoretical* reason) could guide our lives. While we can't *know* freedom (in *reality as it is*), we must *think* freedom is real. We can't ever *know* that there's an afterlife (with rewards for good choices and punishments for evil decisions), but we must *assume* there is. We can't *know* that God exists (in *reality as it is*), but we can *posit* that God exists. So in practical reason, we must assume the nature of reality as it is. We *must* posit what we do in fact posit about *reality as it is* for practical reasons. We need to assume these ideas, even though we can't technically know them, because they help us live good lives.

But Kant's distinction between *reality as it is* and *reality as it appears* opened a door to a deeper skepticism. One interpretation of Kant concludes that our pictures of God are rooted in our own needs, desires, and feelings. So-called knowledge of God isn't really knowledge about God as God really is. Human knowledge of God is no more than knowledge of the human self. Put it another way: There might be no God to shape our religious beliefs. Religious passions manufacture our thoughts about God. The idea of God is an invention, a human projection.

Following this logic, Sigmund Freud (1856-1939) interpreted the idea of God as a psychologically inspired father-image. Emotional weaklings project their desire for a heavenly father-figure, a celestial security blanket, into the heavens. This is how all convictions about God develop. And Karl

Marx (1818-1883) claimed that the bourgeois class (the financial elite who owned all property) created concepts about God in order to hold down the proletariat class (the poor and destitute workers). So religion is the "opiate of the people." If the poor really believe the illusion that their station in life is God's will for them, they become numbed to the effects of their poverty. In the writings of these two powerfully influential men, supposed knowledge of God isn't really knowledge of some *reality as it is* at all. According to Freud and Marx, believing in God is like believing in the Tooth Fairy.

Kant's Copernican Revolution set up postmodern thinking in this way: He believed that all human minds are structured in one, universal way. He assumed that all persons have the same categories in their minds as any self-respecting eighteenth-century Prussian philosopher! If this were right, then all persons would see things in the same way. With a fixed and universal set of mental concepts, all persons would arrive at the same conclusions. And so it seemed to Kant that he'd answered skepticism.

But what if different people have different mental categories? In the centuries since Kant, Western people came to believe that the categories of the human mind can differ widely from time to time and place to place. People today often think that the structure of each individual human mind is forged by a person's unique experience of living in a particular culture and speaking a particular language. The concepts each person uses to see and interpret the world aren't universal and common to all humans. This idea of universal mental structures is a vestige of modernity. Postmodern people believe that our mental categories are particular and specific, grounded in history and tradition. Cultures pass on categories because these structures are embedded in each and every language. Different languages view the world through completely different structures. And thus speakers of different native languages just don't describe the world in identical ways. All people view the world through the lens of their own languages.

Scholars use the phrase, *linguistic turn*, to describe this new sensitivity to the variety of categories built into different languages. *Linguistic turn* describes a fundamental shift in how people look at the *source* or *origin* of the categories or structures by which a person interprets the world. People make the linguistic turn when it suddenly dawns on them that we all see the world through the categories that are unique to our own native tongues. A culture makes a linguistic turn when it becomes widely believed as obviously true that there's no *single human reason* shared by all. To use a computer analogy, not everyone uses Windows 98. Some use completely different operating systems like Unix. Similarly, given the linguistic turn, English and Swahili aren't just distinct languages; they're radically different systems of thought.

Once people or cultures make the linguistic turn, they renounce *universal reason* and celebrate a smorgasbord of *particular forms of logic*. The linguistic turn pushes the Skeptical Question beyond a modernist stance into the postmodern orientation. So Kant's philosophy, modified by those who followed him, aids and abets postmodern skepticism. If *knowledge* means *true beliefs about the "way things really are,"* many in the postmodern world will say that we have *no knowledge at all.* Not only do we have no knowledge of God; we even lack knowledge of the physical world. This surprising conclusion is central to postmodern skepticism.

Flowing into the vacuum created by the postmodern rejection of absolute truth is an adaptation of a nineteenth-century philosophy. Although postmodern types reject the suggestion that they have any philosophy at all, they often borrow what some have called America's one true contribution to philosophy, *pragmatism*. Pragmatism defines truth, not as whatever properly represents reality, but as *whatever works*. Of course, postmodern pragmatists quickly affirm that sometimes it's *useful* to define the word *truth* as a *representation of reality*. For example, the true statement, "I am sitting on a chair," does refer to *reality* in some sense. But for the postmodern pragmatist, a statement isn't true because it corresponds to reality. It's true if someone finds it useful to believe.

Although postmodern pragmatism has a distinctive look and feel, it still emphasizes the connection between truth and usefulness. Contemporary philosopher, Richard Rorty, provides a clear example of this attitude. Rorty doesn't give a series of steps to find knowledge. Unlike Descartes, Rorty has no proper method to suggest. He thinks the Skeptical Question in its modern form, with its concern for evidence and proof, is utterly misplaced. He's careful not to ask, *in the traditional sense*, whether it's the wrong question. Instead of debating the evidence for the modern theory, he just asks whether the modern theory is useful. Since he thinks it isn't, he rejects it as *false*—that is, the theory isn't very useful. Who then decides whether a theory or idea is useful? We arrive at these judgments communally, says Rorty. So he defines *truth* as "what our peers let us get away with saying."

Two other contemporary thinkers have made important contributions to postmodern thought. Jacques Derrida is suspicious of any claim to ultimate truth. He uses a philosophical program—called *Deconstruction*—to make his point. In Derrida's hands, Deconstruction "pokes holes" in the idea that language can convey objective truths about reality. Behind Deconstruction is a strong attitude of suspicion—a tendency to disbelieve—that is rooted in the inclination to see all language as metaphor. Metaphor is figurative language in which one thing is compared to another. For instance, someone might say, "This car is a tin can." If all language is metaphor, this means that language always refers to *other language*, and not to *reality itself.* Thus, Derrida creates ironic, playful arguments in which he gives counter-examples intending to show that there's no completely clear relation, no universal connection, between language and reality.

Michel Foucault ("foo-**koh**") takes the postmodern critique of truth a step further. Foucault argues that because our knowledge is embedded in radically different cultures and languages, the very concept of objective truth about a real world is fallacious. So why do people *pretend* to pursue truth? Following Marx, Foucault says people make truth claims about the world because these claims give them power. Marx said the rich use the idea of truth to pacify the poor. The rich try to pacify the oppressed poor by proclaiming, "The social structure that produced your poverty is God's will!" Thus, the doctrines of the rich give power to the rich in their campaign to keep the poor satisfied in their poverty. Knowledge claims amount to aggression. *Truth-claims* become means to ends, and the ends always involve privilege and power. Comprehensive world-views become slick covers for political agendas. For this reason, any total picture of reality, any comprehensive theory that supposedly explains everything, should arouse suspicion. Surprisingly, skepticism is no longer the unhappy consequence of a failed search for truth; for postmodernism, it's a preferred tool for protecting the downtrodden. Thus, postmoderns always ask: What is the power interest, the political agenda, that lies behind this communication?

This all leads to the Skeptical Question in its postmodern form. Postmodern skepticism doesn't focus exclusively on religious beliefs. Rorty and his postmodern compatriots even-handedly undercut *every* claim to knowledge in the traditional sense. Postmodern skepticism, therefore, is a suspicion of the ability to transcend our individual beliefs, standards, hopes, and dreams. It's a strong tendency to suspect all knowledge claims, to respond to all beliefs with a snide, "Whatever!" Major themes include the grounding of all knowledge claims in usefulness alone (Rorty), the metaphorical nature of language (Derrida), and the intrinsic relationship between knowledge claims and power agendas (Foucault). For the postmodern skeptic, claims to knowledge are nothing more than individual preferences which conceal attempts to gain power and express no more than what is useful for a person—or a group of friends—to believe.

In sum, several key theses express the postmodern stance on knowledge. Taken together, these theses represent the postmodern form of the Skeptical Question.

Historical/cultural/linguistic relativism: The postmodern consciousness emerged from a growing realization that historical and cultural factors affect what we take as valuable, what we think we know, and the standards we set for value and knowledge. This sensitivity to the historical and cultural embeddedness of knowledge profoundly affects the postmodern view of language. In the hands of the postmodern, language ceases to function as a vehicle to represent the world. For the postmodern person, these historical, cultural, and linguistic factors unite to undercut and call into question any claim to knowledge in the traditional sense.

Denial of absolutes/metanarratives: Because knowledge claims are rooted in history, culture, and language, postmodern people claim that all appeals to ultimate truth are impossible (epistemically) and inappropriate (morally). There's just no such thing as "*the* way the world is." There are merely individual accounts or stories ("narratives") of the way we see the world. But there is no one true total theory of complete explanation—no "metanarrative" that explains or gives context to all other stories.

Pragmatism: The demise of ultimate truth leaves a knowledge vacuum. If there is no all-encompassing metanarrative which tells us "*the* way things are," then how do we decide what is good, what is valuable, what should be believed, what should be taken as true? The postmodern answer is: "Whatever works."

The modernist skeptic rejects religious knowledge because it fails to get over the very high crossbar that science supposedly clears. The postmodern skeptic renounces all traditional knowledge claims, whether religious or scientific. So the Skeptical Question in its postmodern form is, "Do we *really* know what we *think* we know since there's no higher viewpoint beyond *your* perspective and *my* perspective?" A postmodern skeptic like Paul (from the case study) would summarize his attitude toward religion in this way: It's naive, arrogant, and oppressive to believe that the Christian God is the one true God and that all other gods are illusions.

ANSWERING *MODERN* SKEPTICISM:

Its Criterion for Knowledge As Too Lofty and Self-Contradictory

Chapter 3

Ideas matter. The attitudes of intellectuals and philosophers work their way into everyday living. For example, I once talked to Pedro, a skillful lawyer from St. Paul who specializes in suing companies for making defective toys. I asked him about religion. He doesn't believe in God, even though his wife does. (His wife really wants him to believe—things would be smoother at home if he did believe—but he just doesn't.) He thinks that if religion works for someone, as it does for his wife, then it's perfectly okay to believe it. But religion isn't for him. Pedro is a typical, contemporary person. He's modern—skeptical about religion, but not about science. (And note: His salary depends on his skepticism about anything that toy companies say about toy safety.) He's also postmodern—relativist, pragmatic, and tolerant. ("If a religion makes good sense to a believer, of course that's fine for the believer, but I just choose not to adopt it.")

What account of knowledge offers a reasonable response to Pedro? Before I offer a response to the modern skeptic and then (in the next chapter) to the postmodern skeptic, let me make three initial points.

First, notice that Pedro bounces back and forth between modern and postmodern versions of the Skeptical Question. Similarly, *many people flip-flop between belief and skepticism.* Like Pedro, people can get quite adamant about proving or criticizing certain beliefs. Meanwhile they hardly blink as they allow other beliefs to slide by unscathed. Certainly we should test and evaluate some of our beliefs; and just as certainly, we can't test and evaluate every belief. But Pedro's approach to knowledge is haphazard. To apply a skeptical attitude to whole classes of beliefs (as Pedro does) is surely wrong-headed. Not everything a toy company says is malicious, and not every religious doctrine is mythology. On the other hand, some corporate claims are malicious, and some religious assertions are false. To sort out good answers to the questions we're facing, we must exercise discipline and consistency.

Second, it follows that skepticism isn't all bad. To avoid the "unexamined life," healthy doubt is good. Doubt is no monster—despite what we may have heard in church—for doubt puts gullibility on a leash. Remember the Heaven's Gate cultists? They thought they would ride to heaven on the tail of the Halle-Bopp Comet. But they didn't ride the comet. They died. They should have doubted their cult leader. They should have listened to their friends' challenge: "Wait a second! Where's your evidence?" An appropriately critical mind helps us examine our lives. It saves us from falling for flimflam con artists. It keeps us from giving money to telephone solicitors who put 90% of our gifts in their pockets and give 10% to the crippled children of St. Paul. Knowing what's true and living according to that truth are important. Socrates was right: "The unexamined life is not worth living."

But *local* skepticism and *global* skepticism are different. Global skepticism doubts every belief whereas healthy local skepticism—call it *critical thinking*—undercuts *some particular* knowledge claims. When I think critically, I certainly don't reject all truth claims out of hand. Rather, by eliminating error, I work my way toward knowledge. In this way, local skepticism is valuable. But global skepticism makes no sense. It assumes that no knowledge is possible. And so it requires, not just doubting con artists, but questioning everyone. Global skeptics will never be taken in, true enough. But it's only because they never believe anything! Rejecting all knowledge means that *global skeptics essentially give equal treatment to the ultra-trustworthy and the completely unreliable*. They distrust both! They don't distinguish an Einstein from a scientific quack. So while local skepticism is highly valuable when it helps in the search for truth, global skepticism is unreasonable.

Third, denying global skepticism doesn't necessarily lead to intolerance. Many in our culture assume that those who claim to know ultimate truth (especially *religious* truth) are *automatically* intolerant. Holding definite beliefs, it is thought, breeds intolerance. But this familiar attitude is flawed for at least three reasons. *First*, while all who are intolerant of others have definite beliefs, the opposite doesn't follow. All 747s are planes, but not all planes are 747s. Not everyone who holds definite beliefs is necessarily intolerant. After all, those who charge religious people with intolerance also hold definite beliefs about the status of religious claims.[3] *Second*, ironically, the commitment to tolerance actually dictates holding to truth. It requires believing that something is *true*, namely, that tolerance is a virtue and intolerance a vice. *Third*, tolerance is an appropriate attitude in a pluralistic society. As a Christian, I believe my atheist friend is wrong. Yet I admit his legal right to hold his view. My friend thinks I am wrong. Yet he admits my right to hold my view. So what's the difference? The search for truth doesn't force either of us to become intolerant.

Now let's move to the question of responding to modern skepticism. What is an effective answer for Mary's father, Peter, the modern skeptic? Recall that Peter doubts God because he thinks that the evidence for God's existence is sub-standard or nonexistent. But notice that behind his rejection of belief in God, Peter assumes an unstated standard for *what properly qualifies as knowledge*. This standard is the ruler by which he measures the evidence for God. Of course, it's probable that people like Peter never really give much thought to this standard. Like the fish that doesn't know it's wet, we all hold basic assumptions that we rarely question. So behind Peter's rejection of God's existence is an *implicit* standard for what rightly counts as genuine knowledge.

In discussing modernism, we identified three fundamental theses of modern religious skepticism: evidentialism, positivism, and scientism. Each of these is an attempt to define what counts as knowledge, an attempt to create a ruler for measuring beliefs to see whether they pass muster. Taken together, these three form a very strict set of criteria for rational belief; in fact, they *equate knowledge with certainty and provability*. But is this a problem? After all, aren't a lot of the problems in this world caused by people believing things they have no good reason to believe? The Ku Klux Klan, for instance, still believes that minorities are destroying America. Certainly, we should counter the influence of false and socially destructive beliefs.

Although we should refute and reject false beliefs, especially when they cause social or personal problems, the skeptics' strict requirements for knowledge aren't acceptable for three reasons. **First,** *if the modernists' criteria for knowledge are correct, much of what is legitimately known would no longer count as knowledge*. For example, I can't prove beyond a shadow of a doubt that the world has existed for more than five minutes. (Maybe it was created, complete with appearance of age, and I came equipped with a full set of life-like memories, only two minutes ago.) I also can't prove that I have a mind. (I might be a cleverly constructed robot—like Commander Data on the TV show *Star Trek: The Next Generation*.) I can't even prove that I love my wife. But do the modernist criteria really show me that I don't know any of these things? Certainly not. The modernist criteria are too high, and while they eliminate all false beliefs, they also rule out many obviously true beliefs. So the criteria are defective. The problem is an overly stringent standard for what constitutes knowledge.

Second, given the first point, *modern skeptics*

tend to cheat; they fail to follow their own rules. The theses of evidentialism, positivism, and scientism can be distilled down into a basic principle, a principle designed to protect the *provability* and *certainty* of all successful claims to knowledge. A general principle of this sort could go something like this:

> *Principle of Knowledge*: Only those beliefs that are *(1) evident to the senses, (2) rationally self-evident (like 1+1=2), or (3) the kind of knowledge to which we have special, guaranteed access* ("I have a pain in my knee") qualify as knowledge.

This principle is intended to ensure the elimination of false beliefs. But there's one problem. Can modern skeptics *know* this Principle of Knowledge? Is this principle itself either evident to the senses, logically self-evident, or the result of special self-knowledge? No! This modernist Principle of Knowledge is inconsistent (in technical terms, *self-referentially incoherent*). That is, the principle is logically equivalent to "Everything I say is a lie" or "I'm not married; just ask my wife." It doesn't meet its own requirement. The net result is something like this: "Everyone has to prove everything—except for my statement that 'Everyone has to prove everything.' I don't have to prove that!"

Things get worse for the modern religious skeptic who trusts science alone! Some modernists turn to science alone as the expression of the hope for knowledge through unvarnished human reason. Arguing for science as the *only* way to knowledge amounts to *scientism*. But scientism commits several fatal mistakes. Here's why. Let me use *s* to designate the statement, "Only scientific statements are rational." The problem is that *s* itself isn't a scientific statement; *s* is a *philosophical* claim about science, not a *scientific* hypothesis about the natural world. So if *s* is *true*, and only scientific statements are rational, then *s*, which isn't a scientific statement, would be irrational and false. In a nutshell, *s* fails its own rule! *The state-*

ment, "All statements must be proved scientifically," can't be proved scientifically.

Scientism makes two other errors. For one thing, *scientism fails to acknowledge that science depends on important assumptions*. Science assumes that an external world exists and that it's orderly, stable, and properly explained by numbers. Science presupposes the laws of logic, mathematics, and language, the general reliability of the human knowing processes, and values like predictive accuracy and simplicity. None of these is provable scientifically. *Further, scientism fails to admit that science is laced with values.* Science can't explain everything by empirical observation alone. Physics may explain the movements of subatomic particles like quarks, but it doesn't explain the decisions of physicists. Those who study quarks are motivated by purposes, and we properly understand their behavior only if we say they value knowledge. Empirical observation can't ground human purposes and values. Humans act purposively, even if quarks don't.

Third, *modern skepticism, when taken as a way of life, a way of living in the world, is very troubling.* We've heard modern skeptics express pride that their agnosticism is intellectually virtuous. They're courageous, not swayed willy-nilly by the winds of contemporary opinion or religious rhetoric. They see themselves as more honest because they stay above the fray, carefully reserving judgment until absolute certainty presents itself. But living life consistently under the principles of skepticism is impossible. Sometimes it's wise to withhold judgment when evidence isn't clear-cut, but we can't withhold judgment about ultimate questions forever.

An illustration suggested by philosopher William James drives home this point. He told of a climber hiking a steep mountain trial. The climber comes to a crevice, too deep to climb into and too wide to jump easily. The climber faces three possible candidates for belief: (1) "I can't jump the crevice; it's too wide," (2) "I can jump the crevice," and (3) "I don't know whether I can jump the crevice." If someone is only *thinking* about the truth of a given belief or statement, then agnosticism—"I just don't know"—seems a viable option. But when it comes to *action*—moving on with one's life—skepticism drops off the map. The climber has only two options about what to do: (1) Try to jump the crevice or (2) turn around and go home.

The same is true with religious belief. If a young woman decides to suspend belief in the existence of God because she thinks the evidence is insufficient or because she doesn't think the time is right, she is in effect rejecting God. Suppose the woman responds with "I don't know" to her boyfriend's marriage proposal. Isn't this matrimonial hesitation *functionally* the same as a "No"? Contrary to what skeptics think, being agnostic about a particular issue often does entail a response to that issue. In the words of the rock music group, *Rush*, "If you choose not to decide, you still have made a choice." Skepticism is the position of "decision by default"—hardly an intellectually virtuous position!

Here's the rub for modern religious skeptics: In order to answer the Skeptical Question, they had set the crossbar of knowledge very high. To avoid erroneous knowledge claims, they carved out tiny, exclusive enclaves in which they sought absolute certainty. (Some of them equated this enclave with science.) But this little ghetto of certitude is too small. It excludes too much. Modernists put the crossbar of knowledge so high that no knowledge claims can clear it, and this means it's impossible to ground any knowledge—*even scientific knowledge*! Ironically, in the very attempt to avoid skepticism, modern philosophers landed right back in skepticism!

ANSWERING *POSTMODERN* SKEPTICISM:

The Possibility of Knowledge Despite Ambiguity and Bias

Chapter 4

What is an appropriate response to Mary's son, Paul, the postmodern skeptic? Postmodern skepticism includes a critique of modern ways of knowing and of modern skepticism, but it goes well beyond modern skepticism by articulating its own variation of the Skeptical Question. Paul holds that because human language and culture shape all knowledge, it's naive to think that there exists an objective truth that all people could find. Paul's suspicion of any ultimate truth means that (1) Mary's definite belief that God exists and (2) Peter's settled conviction that God doesn't exist are *both* wrong-headed. From Paul's perspective, both his mother and grandfather are simple-minded at best and arrogant at worst.

Before we mention the flaws in this disconcerting postmodern stance, however, we must point out that the postmodern critique is right about several things. The postmodern person correctly reminds us that pursuing absolute rational certainty is misguided. For this reason, equating knowledge and certainty will doom our search for truth. In addition, historical and cultural factors do shape what we think we know, and much of the language we use is subject to misinterpretation—there's no such thing as *one* obvious meaning for each single sentence.

These insights are correct, but full-blown postmodern skepticism takes several serious missteps. *First, nothing we've cited about the cultural, linguistic, or historical nature of human knowledge implies—or even slyly suggests—that knowledge is not important, not possible, or not necessary.* Knowledge of ambiguity doesn't prove that *all* knowledge is ambiguous.[4] While we're aware of some things about which we can't be clear, this doesn't show that everything is unclear. There's a very important difference between the claim that attempting to acquire knowledge is *difficult* and the claim that all such attempts are *doomed to failure, impossible, or morally inappropriate.*

Second, the idea of truth—the traditional notion of truth as what corresponds to reality—*is not easily discarded.* Representative postmodern skeptics like Rorty, Derrida, and Foucault, whatever else they want to do, certainly want to undercut this traditional definition of *truth*. But it's still right to ask: In what sense do Derrida and Foucault, with their respective criticisms of the concept of truth, believe their criticisms are *true*? Suppose they adopt Rorty's notion of "truth as usefulness." Then Derrida and Foucault are saying their claims are *true* because they're *useful for them*. But would this mean that anyone who judges that these claims are *not* useful may readily dispense with those critiques? Or maybe Derrida and Foucault mean that their critique really is objectively useful *for all people*. But doesn't this amount to saying that it's *true* (in the sense of *corresponding to reality*) that their critique is useful for all people? Try though they may, the traditional notion of truth defies elimination and redefinition. Regarding *anyone's* attempt to eliminate or redefine *truth*, we may always ask: What about this new definition? Is it true in the sense that *this* is the way truth really is?

Third, the postmodern analysis of power and its relation to truth is stated too strongly. Foucault built a career on showing how claims to knowledge in various contexts are merely poorly concealed attempts to usurp power or maintain privilege. We grant Foucault's claim: Many knowledge claims do have power implications. Sometimes knowledge claims have a very minimal and localized connection with power. For example, one roommate says to the other, "It's your turn to take out the garbage, because I did it last time." At other times there is a more significant and pervasive connection between knowledge and power. For instance, a presidential candidate claims to be the best nominee and says, "The Democratic Party has the right agenda for the American nation."

But the intrinsic connection between knowledge claims and power doesn't necessarily *disprove* any belief. Noticing the fact that power attaches itself to knowledge claims doesn't help us decide whether knowledge claims in general or any one claim in particular is *false*. Here are some examples. Take a statement with almost zero power implications: "This flower is red." Does the fact that this statement can't produce or support much power make the claim true? Certainly not! Now consider an assertion with obvious power implications: "I am the best candidate for the presidency." Does the enormous power implication necessarily make this claim false? Not by a long shot. Maybe the person running for president *really is*, without any doubt, the best candidate. So greater or lesser power implications of some assertion don't directly correlate with higher or lower probability of the claim's being true.

Fourth, and even worse, Foucault's protestations about the connection between knowledge and power also indict the postmodern stance. This snake bites its own tail. If all assertions harbor power agendas, then the postmodern critique is also an attempt to advance some particular agenda. A person told me, "Every attempt at persuasion is an act of violence." This person apparently failed to see that he was trying to persuade me of this point.

A profound illustration of this comes in the writings of Rorty. Responding to philosopher Hilary Putnam's objections about Rorty's critique of traditional notions of truth, Rorty says,

> Let me just grant that, in some suitably broad sense, I *do* want to substitute new concepts for old. I want to recommend

> explaining "better" (in the context "better standards of warranted assertability") as "will come to seem better to us" . . . Nor can I see what "us" can mean here except: us educated, sophisticated, tolerant, wet liberals, the people who are always willing to hear the other side, to think out all the implications, etc.—the sort of people, in short, who Putnam and I hope, at our best, to be.[5]

The standards for truth and knowledge, according to Rorty, aren't decided by all. Only sophisticated liberals get a voice. Evidently, poor uneducated people don't count. The voice of political conservatives is ignored. And Christians? Well, Rorty thinks that Christians (at least those who *really* believe in Christianity) are insane and consequently shouldn't be allowed to take part in liberal society, and perhaps should even be forced to undergo therapy until they achieve (Rorty's brand of) enlightenment. Now isn't this a blatant use of "knowledge" on the part of one particular group to gain control over another? If we take the postmodern critique that all knowledge claims conceal power ploys, and we apply that critique to all knowledge claims, then the critique indicts itself. In sum, some assertions are attempts to acquire power. True enough. But this insight, correct though it is, doesn't disprove all knowledge claims.

Fifth, pragmatism's replacement for truth, the concept of usefulness, *just doesn't capture what most people mean when they say that something "is true."* Truth and usefulness do sometimes coincide, but what's useful isn't necessarily true, and what's true isn't always useful. On the one hand, *not all useful claims are true.* Take the belief, prevalent in Nazi Germany in the 1930s: "Particular ethnic groups, particularly Jews, are responsible for Germany's economic woes." This proved very effective for Hitler who used it to whip up war fever and to end Germany's depression and create a booming, wartime economy. But it's false. The actual causes of Germany's economic hardships in the 1930s were much more complicated, being connected, for instance, with America's Great Depression. On the other hand, *not all true beliefs are useful.* The puppy I received for my 13th birthday was 2 1/4 pounds at six weeks of age. This is true, but it's virtually useless to me—and absolutely pointless to anyone else. (After all, it was my dog!) So we just can't equate truth with usefulness.

Finally, for all its objections to modern skepticism, it seems that (at least certain varieties) *of postmodern skepticism really assume the truth of certain key tenets of modernism.* Postmodern skepticism goes something like this: "Since all knowledge is rooted in cultures and languages and since pure objectivity and certainty aren't possible, we must conclude that all knowledge is subjective. Thus, we should discard the idea of truth as correspondence." But the question is: Why assume that we must achieve complete objectivity and certainty before we have genuine knowledge? This assumption is borrowed from a tradition that goes all the way back to Descartes and beyond. Ironically, it's an aspect of modernism that postmodernism sometimes fails to lay aside.

Here's the rub for the postmodern skeptic: Realizing that some people use their rhetoric to gain political influence, postmodern people responded by deconstructing—poking holes in—all truth claims and metanarratives (the comprehensive stories that explain everything). Postmodern people tend to see metanarratives as naive, arrogant, and oppressive. But it's impossible to get away from truth claims. If the postmodern claim is that *all* metanarratives should be mistrusted, they are themselves making a universal claim—a claim we should presumably mistrust. Granted, power does drive some metanarratives, some comprehensive theories about the world. But this by itself isn't sufficient to undercut the notion that truth and knowledge are attainable. Perhaps a true metanarrative does exist. If it does, we are wise to seek it.

So even though some today see skepticism as

somehow more virtuous, courageous, or honest than believing in something as true, we have seen that there are significant flaws in the skeptical denial of truth and knowledge. So perhaps we can now accept Socrates' point: Knowledge *is* a treasure worth seeking. But a negative critique of skepticism isn't the same as a positive plan for discovering this treasure. What, then, is required to arrive at genuine knowledge? In the remaining chapters we'll see how it's possible to *move beyond skepticism to genuine knowledge*. We'll look at what truth and knowledge are: how we form and test beliefs: the necessity of knowing virtuously; and the possiblility of religious knowledge.

TRUTH AND KNOWLEDGE:

Knowledge As True Belief Held by a Person for an Appropriate Reason

Chapter 5

It's critical to distinguish *truth* and *knowledge.* These two concepts are often equated, with chaotic results. But truth and knowledge are different concepts. Put simply, *true affirmations* are those which correspond to reality, and so *truth* is a characteristic of statements that properly describe aspects of the real world. This is called the *correspondence theory of truth.* The correspondence theory of truth isn't a method for testing truth claims or discovering knowledge. It's a definition of what we mean when we say that a statement "is true." According to the correspondence theory, what makes a statement *true* is reality itself. A statement like, "This car is red," is true, simply if the car in question actually is red. So truth doesn't depend on anyone *knowing* the truth. Even if no one's around to discover that it's 115° on August 15, 1977 at 2:00 p.m. in the middle of Death Valley, it's still true that it's 115° out in that desert. The statement, "It's 115° on August 15, 1977 at 2:00 p.m. in the middle of Death Valley," is still true even if no one thinks about it. Truth is independent of human minds.

The word *knowledge* denotes a person's proper understanding of the true nature of reality. This proper grasping of reality can be *knowledge by acquaintance.* In this sense, I know what the color blue looks like. An accurate perception of reality can also take the form of *knowledge of true statements* that describe that reality. Both of these are important. Knowing a friend is more akin to knowing by acquaintance, and it's more important than just knowing about a friend. But knowing true statements is also important. In fact, the two kinds of knowing are related, because knowing by acquaintance entails the truth of descriptive statements. Knowing a friend named Greg entails knowing many true propositions, like "Greg exists" and "I count Greg as a friend."

For a belief to count as knowledge for a person, it must meet three conditions. *First, knowledge must be* ***true***. I don't just mean that someone *thinks* the idea is true. I mean that it *is* true. Members of the Flat Earth Society (believe it or not, there is such a thing!) *think* that the earth is flat. Do we count their belief as knowledge? Of course not! They *believe* the earth is flat, but their belief is false and hence doesn't count as knowledge. Genuine knowledge is *true*.

Second knowledge must be ***believed***. I have to believe a claim (that is, I have to think that it's true) in order to know it. Of course, believing something isn't enough to *make it true*, and not believing it doesn't *make it false*. But without belief, a true idea isn't knowledge for that person. Suppose it's true that one of my great-great-grandfathers was a Confederate Army lieutenant whose troops played a key role at the Battle of Fredericksburg. Now suppose I have no particular beliefs about this person. In this case, it's obviously *true* that my great-great-grandfather was this lieutenant, but it would be very odd to say that I *know* this about my great-great-grandfather. In fact, I probably have very few beliefs about my great-great-grandfathers. Perhaps I know generic things, such as: Eight persons who lived sometime in the last 250 years are my great-great-grandfathers. They were males; they fathered my great-grandparents; and none of them ever received e-mail. But since I don't *believe* anything individually about any of them, I can't be said to *know* anything distinctive about them as individuals. I have to *believe* something to know it.

Third, knowledge requires ***some other fact*** *that legitimates the knower's holding that belief.* The belief must arise out of this legitimating fact; it must be based on this "something else." The exact nature of this legitimating fact is hotly debated. But the importance of this legitimating account is that it separates genuine knowledge from beliefs that are true purely by chance. Obviously, we shouldn't consider a true belief as knowledge if that belief was the result of a wild guess. Say I win the lottery by guessing the winning numbers. Sure, I *hoped* that the winning numbers would be 10 15 20 25 30, but it's wrongheaded to say that I *knew* that they would be the winning numbers! In sum, by the word *knowledge*, we mean a true belief held by a person for an appropriate reason.

FORMING AND TESTING BELIEFS:

Particularism, Rationality, and Evidence

Chapter 6

If knowledge is true belief plus some legitimating fact, a major question is this: How should we set the standards for assessing these legitimating facts? Descartes was obsessed with this very problem, and his philosophy set the stage for the modern discussions of knowledge. Remember that Descartes' approach posited very high—too high—standards for that "something else," that legitimating fact that turns merely true belief into genuine knowledge.

In order to weed out false beliefs and gain genuine knowledge, Descartes required that all candidates for genuine knowledge must arise from a method. Correct method—for Descartes it was the geometric method—is key to finding true knowledge. This approach is called *methodism*. Methodism, in this discussion, isn't a religious denomination. Rather it's an epistemic theory that stipulates this: Someone knows any *particular* true belief only if he arrived at that knowledge by following a correct *method*. Here's a specific case. Suppose I ask whether I know the statement, "My coffee cup is blue." (Let's call this statement *p*.) Methodism would require that before I can know *p*, I must *follow a proper method* by which I know *p*. In sum, to know any particular truth, I must follow a proper method.

Although Descartes' methodism may seem like a promising way to ground knowledge, it's fundamentally flawed. Methodism requires that before I can know anything, I must have *prior knowledge* of the method by which to know that thing. But then how do I know that method itself? My coming to know what method to use would itself require following a prior method. This quickly leads to what's called an infinite regress. Every time I try to answer the problem, the problem keeps appearing. I start moving back a chain of questions. But every time I move back to a prior link in the chain, the problem repeatedly emerges. It's like asking, "What explains Michael's existence?" If I say, "His parents," I just raise again the very question I hoped to answer: "What explains his parents' existence?" "Their parents?" Ultimately, given the methodist approach, there's no way to end this infinite series of questions.

But there's another approach to finding the legitimating fact that turns true belief into knowledge. It's called *particularism.* Particularism starts by *assuming* that we do know things since we find that we already know many *particular* things. In certain conditions, we typically form true beliefs—beliefs formed through a variety of means. We see a tree or hear a train. We compute things. We infer conclusions from things we see or hear. We learn from experts. Each of these processes generally leads to true beliefs. And so it's legitimate to count these particular beliefs as knowledge. We don't have to step back and first prove that, say, our vision is perfect, before we believe something we see. That would lead us back to the methodist trap (since I'd have to prove the method by which I proved my vision is perfect.) So it's better just to assume that our properly formed beliefs are innocent until proven guilty. With these particular beliefs in hand as examples, we can begin to understand what knowledge is—and gradually to increase the number of things we know.

But difficulties arise when we run into contrary evidence. Let's say I know, just by looking at it, that a particular stick is straight. I have no reason to doubt this because my eyesight's generally very good. Then I put the stick in water, and suddenly it appears bent. I know that the stick can't be both straight and bent. So which of my two visual experiences is right? Or let's say my wife helps me pick out a tie that looks gray to me. I protest: "It's too drab." But she assures me that the tie is a nice shade of rose. Should I trust her judgment?

When this sort of thing happens, we go back to testing procedures that help us figure out which of the things our belief-forming processes are telling us is actually correct. The conflict between these normally reliable indicators leads us to question whether what we think we saw could really be so. I remember something in my high school physics class about light refracting when it passes through water, and this accounts for the bent appearance. Or I remember that I'm color blind in reds and greens, and this explains why the rose-colored tie looks gray to me. So what do we do about conflicting facts. Do we just give up and concede skepticism? Hardly.

We follow several specific strategies to evaluate important beliefs. *First, our beliefs should be rational.* At a minimum, this means that our beliefs shouldn't contradict one another. This is *coherence*, a negative test. Say I believe both that "I am the world's leading microbiologist" and that "I don't know much about microbiology." These beliefs are obviously incompatible, and so holding both beliefs at the same time is irrational: One of the two (or maybe both) must go. Coherence is necessary, but it doesn't guarantee truth. But incoherence is a significant red flag. It *guarantees* that some beliefs are false, and we would do well to avoid holding incoherent beliefs.

Second, our beliefs should fit with the evidence. If a belief doesn't fit with a whole host of data we take to be true, we have good reason to think that belief is false. Take the belief, "I'm the sixteenth president of the United States." This belief conflicts with other well-established facts: "The sixteenth U.S. president's name was Abraham Lincoln"; "My name is Bob Garcia"; "Abraham Lincoln is dead"; "I'm alive"; and so on. Generally, we look for beliefs that fit the evidence. But notice something very important. We don't stipulate a rule: "Every belief must be proved by evidence before it counts as knowledge." That rule would force us back to evidentialism, and that's an intellectual cul-de-sac. Although knowledge is obviously possible without a strict evidentialist requirement, we still recognize that evidence is important and helpful in determining which beliefs should count as knowledge, especially in cases where generally reliable beliefs conflict.

We've been talking about *particular beliefs*. But we also seek knowledge about large *networks of truth-claims*. A large-scale scientific theory, for example, is a complex set of interlocking claims, all connected in a large web of beliefs. Large-scale models include many different kinds of things, including scientific, historical, and even religious convictions.

Large-scale models compete with each other to see which one does the best job of explaining all the facts. Thus, for instance, the heliocentric (sun-centered) model of our solar system competed with the geocentric (earth-centered) model. Though this isn't well-known, it's actually true that for centuries, both the heliocentric and geocentric models explained the available physical facts equally well. Physical observations didn't finally confirm the heliocentric model until more than 200 years after Galileo's controversies. Thus the heliocentric model didn't compete with the facts. Rather, it competed with and finally defeated the geocentric model of the solar system by doing a better job of explaining the most facts. This is one way large-scale models gain support—by outdoing their rivals at explaining the data.

Here's another example. When National Transportation Safety Board (NTSB) investigators are trying to explain a plane crash, they look for evidence. They know what to look for because they've explained other crashes and have found telltale facts that guide them to large-scale explanations. The telltale facts are clues that unlock patterns of interpretation and lead to strongly supported explanations. The NTSB will put together all the data and conclude, say, that the plane crashed because a turbine fin in one of the engines broke apart. The power of this explanation to incorporate all the relevant data—like the loud explosion and the sudden loss of airspeed reported by the cockpit data recorder —is a major reason we hold that the large-scale theory is a properly-supported, interlocking set of true beliefs. The individual facts are themselves grounded in experience such as the sound of the explosion and the report of the planes reduced airspeed). The large-scale theory incorporates and explains these and many other facts.

Complex explanatory models can form ongoing programs of research and investigation. They not only explain what we know already; they can also guide us to what we don't yet know. Take, for example, the discovery of Neptune. Uranus didn't orbit the sun as the large-scale models suggested it should. But when scientists supposed that another planet was exerting gravitational force on Uranus, then its orbit suddenly made sense. So scientists began looking for this other planet, and eventually they found Neptune. This is similar to "superstring theory" which developed when theorists used mathematics to explain their observations! The mathematical calculations worked out beautifully when scientists assumed the existence of things they called superstrings. The calculations are powerful in that they explain a number of related issues. So researchers posit that superstrings exist even though they can't observe them. Research programs that guide researchers to new discoveries are progressive. This helps confirm their connection with the real world.

But testing large-scale constellations of beliefs isn't simple. In fact, it's sometimes impossible. Theories about particular events, like why a particular ship went down in a perfectly calm sea, may never in fact be understood. The problem might be that certain key pieces of evidence are stuck too far down on the sea floor. This means we could explain the event *in principle*, but not *in fact*. That is, there's no logical reason why we can't explain this event, but there is a physical barrier to our explaining it. So in this case, we should better remain agnostic rather than claim to know what we really can't know—at least until we develop a new submersible vessel that can get down to the wreck and find the key evidence. The truth about some complex processes might be just as hidden.

Testing models is complex because it requires making judgments of several different kinds. What are the facts to be explained? (Sometimes the two models will explain different ranges of data, and there's often no way to step outside the two models to know which range of apparent facts is really most relevant.) What are the criteria by which we decide which explanation is best? (Sometimes the two explanations will excel at two different criteria—one model might be simpler while the other is more helpful in guiding us to new discoveries.) So these procedures aren't straightforward and linear. But reasonable judgments are still possible. When the NTSB investigators find a cracked turbine fin, we know we shouldn't blame the pilots for the crash (and maybe we should blame the aircraft manufacturers). Gathering knowledge isn't always easy, but it's amazing how much we can learn through carefully using all the strategies we have available.

KNOWLEDGE AND THE INTELLECTUAL VIRTUES:

The Importance of How *We Come To Know*

Chapter 7

Thus far, we've been discussing some of the key elements of a proper understanding of knowledge, including belief formation and testing. We've shown that knowledge requires true belief plus some account of that belief, something that legitimates the belief. But thus far we've been quite coy about what this account is. It's time—indeed, past time—to repair that deficiency.

What is this feature that, when added to true belief, constitutes knowledge? Here scholars disagree—in fact, there are few things about which they disagree more! Thankfully, it's not my purpose to address all the academic squabbles. Rather, we'll offer an account of knowledge that avoids the Skeptical Question in both of its varieties. The account we find most persuasive focuses on the relationship between knowledge and the *intellectual virtues*.

What are intellectual virtues, and how do they fit in with an understanding of knowledge? Intellectual virtues share some characteristics with moral virtues. In fact, many acts that are virtuous in a moral context are also virtuous in an intellectual context. Examples of intellectual virtues are honesty and courage. Being intellectually honest means making a fair appraisal of the evidence at hand, dedicating effort to reaching all conclusions, admitting personal biases that affect beliefs, and seeking to override or reduce those biases. In an intellectual context, courage involves, among other things, being willing to take minority positions when the evidence points in that direction. It also requires investigating personal beliefs with rigor.

An intellectual virtue, therefore, is a characteristic of a person who acts in a praiseworthy manner in the process of forming beliefs. But an epistemic *virtue* isn't simply an instance of intellectual *skill*. For example, think about the ability to see colors sharply. This is a skill that some lucky people have from birth. Since this ability isn't developed over time, it's not particularly virtuous. Virtue relates more to what a person *does with* abilities or skills like incredibly sharp vision.

Further, the intellectual virtues don't happen naturally. Rather, they arise from habits. Like good habits (such as exercising and eating healthfully) and bad habits (like biting fingernails and gossiping), the intellectual virtues are the sorts of things that become more and more a part of us the more we practice them. Similarily, the more we practice their opposites, like intellectual dishonesty, the more difficult it becomes to respond to any given situation in an intellectually virtuous way.

Intellectual virtues connect directly to the motivations of the one employing them. A person must come to believe something out of proper intentions. Say that a student named John hears a teacher talking about a classmate John particularly dislikes. "He is nice," the teacher says. Because of his ill-will toward the student, John hears, "He has lice." Even if it's true that the student has lice, does John's belief count as knowledge? No. Even if he believes it, it's true, and it's grounded in a normally reliable belief-forming process (John has good hearing), from a virtue perspective, John's belief doesn't count as knowledge since this belief arose in an intellectually non-virtuous way. John's belief was affected by his malicious attitude toward the fellow student. Given all these points, therefore, we define *knowledge* in this way: Knowledge is *true belief which is reached or acquired through an act of virtue.*[6]

How does this account of knowledge help us respond to the two Skeptical Questions? Recall Peter's insistence that Mary's belief must be accompanied by evidence. Modern skepticism is fixated on the adequacy of a person's evidence. The key insight of virtue epistemology is that knowledge isn't just an issue of whether evidence exists for specific belief at a particular time, but an issue of *how a person goes about gathering evidence*. So whether or not a particular belief is properly grounded for me has to do with how I formed the belief. Did I form this belief in accord with the intellectual virtues, reflecting praiseworthy habits of belief formation and testing acquired over time? Or did I form this belief in a manner that reflected slipshod handling of the evidence or haphazard reasoning processes? The notion of evidence is still important, but more important is *whether we rightly handle the evidence we have*!

An emphasis on the intellectual virtues also helps us answer the postmodern skeptical challenge. Remember that Paul emphasized the problems that compromise all knowledge claims: the historical/cultural background of all knowledge, the metaphorical nature of language, and the intrinsic relationship between knowledge and power. The insight behind Paul's objections is that the evidence for many different beliefs—some complex, some mundane—isn't obvious. An unscrupulous person can twist evidence to support the position he holds. But an intellectually virtuous person, someone who's not unscrupulous, will operate differently. If a man is intellectually virtuous, he will treat evidence honestly, overcome his biases toward his own culture, and refuse to misuse evidence to gain power or to pretend that his own pet beliefs are superior.

Those possessing intellectual virtue will do what they can to transcend their historical and cultural location, even though this is never completely possible. Virtuous people can and do work to understand the viewpoints others hold, most of all through dialogue with those who actually hold those different views. Of course, history is full of examples where this didn't happen. But this only says that history is filled with intellectually non-virtuous people—not a surprising conclusion.

So is knowledge possible? Yes! The existence of junk car yards doesn't count as an argument against the existence of new cars. Similarly, the existence of intellectually non-virtuous people doesn't show that intellectually virtuous people fail completely in their quest for genuine knowledge. In sum, due to human limits, some things are beyond knowing. But if we exercise the intellectual virtues, we can achieve genuine knowledge about important things. Skepticism wins some skirmishes along the way, but it doesn't win the war!

RELIGIOUS KNOWLEDGE:

Finding Standards Suitable to the Knowledge of God

Chapter 8

Humans *can* attain knowledge, even though it's sometimes difficult. Knowledge is best seen as arising from the operation of intellectual virtues such as honesty, courage, open-mindedness, and conviction. But what about religious knowledge or belief in God? Can we arrive at genuine knowledge of God if we act in an intellectually virtuous manner? Certainly yes!

Let us get one idea clear at the start: Rejecting all religious knowledge *just because it's religious* is sheer prejudice. This is called a *demarcation strategy*. Those who use demarcation strategies try to draw a boundary between whole classes of knowledge for the purpose of rejecting one whole class of beliefs. Such strategies require distinguishing supposedly legitimate (usually scientific) knowledge claims from illegitimate (often religious) ones. But such strategies are doomed. Identifying the dividing line between the supposedly true class and the allegedly false or meaningless class has proved impossible. There's no neat and tidy demarcation line between different classes of beliefs. Invariably, demarcation strategies rule out either too much or too little. Not every religious idea is false, and not every supposedly scientific proposal is true.

Rather than attempting to come up with a single rule to handle all knowledge claims or attempting to determine what *classes* of knowledge are legitimate, it's better to test *individual* claims one by one. In so doing, we may very well find certain religious beliefs—say, beliefs held by Heaven's Gate cult members who drank poison so they could ride the Halle-Bopp Comet—worthy of complete and utter rejection. (We may also find quackery—say, the claim that taking a certain pill will help you lose 50 pounds in a week—disguised as scientific knowledge.) Still, none of this shows that well-supported religious beliefs should be discounted *just because they're religious.*

But isn't the existence of God something fundamentally different than the existence of trees, koala bears, and supernovae? After all, trees, koala bears, and supernovae are directly observable whereas we can't put God in a test tube and analyze him. Of course, we know some things that aren't directly observable. For example, there's an infinite number of decimal places in *pi*, and love is a virtue, not a vice. Still it seems God should make his existence more obvious. Why doesn't he? This question is often labeled the *hiddenness of God* problem, a difficult question that threatens to take us into deep and muddy waters. But it's so important that we must at least sketch an answer.[7]

One insight will help us here: Some kinds of knowledge are just more obvious than others. Imagine Jill's experience of putting her hand on a stove and finding that it's really hot. In this case, what counts as genuine knowledge is pretty hard to miss. Truth of this sort is right in Jill's face; it takes little virtue to learn this, for the ability to sense heat is hardwired in the human body. But with more complex kinds of knowledge, what's really true is easier to miss. Truth of this sort is more subtle; it takes developed virtue to learn it. For example, scientists failed to recognize the stray marks on photographic plates *as important* until their theory told them to start looking for certain subatomic particles. After their theory suggested the possibility of those particles, the scientists realized they already had the evidence on their photographic plates. They just didn't recognize the evidence because it wasn't obvious at first, and they hadn't yet learned what to look for. Analogously, with certain kinds of knowledge, we have to *learn how to learn.*

Then what sort of evidence *is* appropriate to religious knowledge—particularly, to knowledge of the Christian God? One problem is that people often give special weight to non-religious forms of evidence. Yuri Gagarin, the celebrated Russian cosmonaut, circled the earth, looked out the window of his space craft, and, seeing no God, came back to earth to proclaim that he'd confirmed atheism. Gagarin was a brave cosmonaut, but not a keen philosopher. (Never mind for the moment that *heaven*, as in the place of God's dwelling, isn't located in the earth's stratosphere.) There's a simple problem here: God isn't the sort of being of whom we should expect a visual sighting. The reality of God's existence is quite clear all around us. But it's not visible to those who aren't motivated or haven't learned to look for it. The insight here is that the evidence we seek must be appropriate to the intended object of knowledge. It's not wise to pretend that the kind of data that point to natural and physical objects is automatically superior to the sort of evidence that reveals spiritual realities.

According to the Bible, the Christian God isn't particularly interested in having people merely believe *that* he exists. Intellectual knowledge of the statement "God exists" is insufficient. In fact, James 2:19 says (in a sarcastic tone worthy of a late-night talk show), "So you believe that God exists? So what! Even the demons believe that" (paraphrase). Instead, the Christian God, wanting what is morally best for us, isn't satisfied to change only our beliefs (even including the belief about whether he exists). The Christian God wants us to depend on him, to trust him, and commit ourselves to him. God doesn't want people to know him in a bland, ho-hum, "Yeah, God exists. So what"? Trusting in God is essential because it's the means by which a relationship with God is established. And God created us to be in relationship with him!

These points mean that we often miss the evidence that we do have. According to the Bible, God did make his presence quite obvious at particular times in history. But people often refused or failed to see God's purposes. For example, in the person of Jesus Christ, God literally walked among the people of Palestine. But in spite of the obviousness of Christ's personal presence, his teachings, and miracles, many people didn't follow him. Remember the time Jesus fed over 5000 people by multiplying a small lunch? Everyone was duly impressed. But instead of recognizing this miracle as a sign of God's presence and making the appropriate moral response, the vast majority latched onto the miracle as a short path to a literally free lunch. When Jesus made it clear that his purposes were far higher than a free lunch program, the crowd drifted away. Here's a case where Jesus made it painfully obvious that something incredible, something divine, was in their midst. But most of his audience wanted lunch, not spiritual transformation. They missed the point—even though they saw the miraculous lunch before their eyes.

What are the reasons people miss evidence? Some failures to see the evidence that points to God's existence may be due to a human knower's personal qualities. My personal characteristics, including attitudes, assumptions, and experiences, can dampen my ability to grasp the evidence that's relevant to a particular kind of knowing. For instance, learning to distinguish the sound of a Stradivarius from the sound of other good violins requires a practiced ear. Someone who never listens to violins won't develop the necessary skills. Similarly, learning to know God intimately requires a level of personal selflessness and moral wisdom, and these are qualities that must be developed.

Other failures to focus on the kind of evidence that there is for God's existence may be due the purposes of a human knower. As knowers we choose to pursue the kinds of knowledge that are important to us. Human values even motivate scientific discovery. Why on earth would someone spend all the time, money, and energy required by scientific research if that person didn't value the results? This means that we must choose whether or not we will follow the path to the most valuable knowledge of all—knowledge of God. If God exists and wants to enter into intimate relationship with me, then rationality and wisdom declare to me in no uncertain terms that I am wise to become the sort of person who can experience this reality. I ought to devote myself to becoming the kind of person who can truly know God. I should make God's purpose my own. The Bible says that the pure in heart see God (Matthew 5:8). Those whose allegiance to God is undivided will know him. So I should put myself in that position—I should develop the needed intellectual virtues—for knowledge of God is the greatest treasure of all.

For those who willingly develop the intellectual virtues, who are willing to look honestly and courageously at the evidence, and who choose knowing God as a value, indications of God's existence are quite surprising. Recently, scientists have learned that the universe is fine-tuned for life. The design parameters for life are very specific. This means that if the forces that hold the universe together varied just slightly—differed by just a couple percentage points or less—then life wouldn't be possible. Our universe may *seem* inhospitable to life. But in fact, only a universe very specifically like this one can produce life.

Take, for example, the strong nuclear force. This force holds atoms together. Without it, atoms would fly apart, and no molecules would form. If this force were 0.3% stronger, life-essential elements would be unstable. If it were 2% weaker, only hydrogen would form. Either way the universe couldn't support life.[8] There are many forces like this, and they're independent of each other. The probability of these independent forces *all* being in the right range is *1* in 10,000,000,000 multiplied by itself 123 times. Talk about stacking the odds! It's hard to avoid honestly concluding that there's strong evidence for an intelligent designer.

Another scientific conclusion is beyond dispute: Living cells are amazingly intricate. Michael Behe, a biochemistry professor, points to the design of living cells in an important book, *Darwin's Black Box.*[9] In Darwin's day, scientists imagined that cells are potatoes, like blobs of stuff inside a thin skin. They saw cells as "black boxes." What happens inside was anyone's guess. But living cells are unimaginably complex. Tiny molecular "machines" haul cargo, fight off attacks, ingest food, and replicate themselves. For instance, a bacterial flagellum (a whip-like propeller) has biochemical parts like bushings, drive shaft, rotor, universal joint, and propeller. And even though cells average one-thousandth of an inch across, each has a command center to guide these machines.

But there's more. The parts of these machines must fit together in a system. Imagine fitting a 12-foot fishing boat with a fighter jet engine. Even if the boat and jet engine are top quality, the two aren't matched. Similarly, all the parts of these molecular machines must work together. If the pieces of the systems aren't coordinated, they won't work. To illustrate, Behe offers a now-famous analogy: the humble mousetrap. Mousetraps have five parts: platform, spring, holding bar, trap hammer, and catch. Each part is designed. Each part fits in the system. Only when all five parts work together will a mousetrap catch mice. Try to make the system "simpler" by taking away any one part, and the trap just won't work. Take away any one piece, and it catches exactly zero mice. Similarly, cells are irreducibly complex. Without all the parts working in a system, none of the parts can do its job. Again, this looks for all the world like intelligent design.

Of course, this amazing complexity of life doesn't *absolutely prove* that God exists as some believed in the past. But evidence like this strongly suggests that denying or ignoring the existence of an intelligent designer is hazardous at best. Even though some fail to see it, the evidence does point to the existence of an intelligent Creator. So if, as millions of believers testify, knowledge of God is the most important thing to acquire, then refusing to consider what it might take to find such knowledge is the height of folly. Deliberately choosing to live a life that leads *away* from truth is a mistake of monumental proportions! Beginning the journey to find genuine knowledge of God is the most reasonable thing to do with our lives.

CONCLUSION

The Skeptical Question has a long history. Some continue to embrace stingy forms of skepticism. They're so intent on avoiding a single false belief that they willingly risk losing the only truth that really matters. These people are feeling the influence of the history of Western ideas. The drift of intellectual thought has moved us toward forms of skepticism that make religious knowledge seem especially troubling and difficult. But these forms of skepticism are severely flawed. So it's acceptable to risk believing an occasional false belief if this opens the door to important truth. Only if we take on the challenge to seek God can we avoid the certainty of knowing very little about him. Hockey superstar Wayne Gretsky once said that 100% of the shots he doesn't take *don't* go in! If we never believe anything, we'll never find truth.

So why should anyone start this journey toward knowledge of God? We've shown why the modern and postmodern skeptical stances no longer block our path. Their high-jump crossbars are unreasonably high. The bars must be lowered, not to the ground, but to a reasonable height. Truth isn't easy to attain, but the journey to truth is worth the effort. And if we live according to truth, if we properly identify that truth and live as God has planned, only then will our deepest longings be fulfilled. C. S. Lewis captures this best:

> If we consider the unblushing promises of reward and the staggering nature of the rewards promised in the Gospels, it would seem that Our Lord finds our desires, not too strong, but too weak. We are half-hearted creatures, fooling about with drink and sex and ambition when infinite joy is offered us, like an ignorant child who wants to go on making mud pies in a slum because he

cannot imagine what is meant by the offer of a holiday at the sea.[10]

The Skeptical Question arose in the West due to a long, meandering series of sometimes well-intentioned, but often ill-conceived intellectual moves. One thing is more clear today than it has been for centuries: It's perfectly reasonable and well-justified to pursue genuine knowledge of the infinite God and of the eternal joy God promises. Those who insist on standing in the skeptical heritage will miss the holiday at the sea.

ENDNOTES

[1]The terms *rationalism* and *empiricism* are rather general categories. Not all philosophers represent one of these ideals exactly since most rationalists include some empirical elements in their theories and vice versa. But some, like David Hume, illustrate a nearly pure form of empiricism.

[2]The logical positivists also allowed that definitions and tautologies are meaningful.

[3]The very definition of *tolerance* is shifting. The word *tolerance* actually means "allowing others to believe differently than you do." In the contemporary distortion of this word, however, it has come to mean "accepting all views as legitimate." But the newer meaning is untenable, and holding the traditional definition is more consistent. Those who use the term in the newer sense aren't tolerant of the view that truth is absolute and genuine knowledge is attainable, for they reject this view as illegitimate.

[4]A phrase borrowed from E. D. Hirsch, *Validity in Interpretation* (New Haven, Conn.: Yale University Press, 1967), ix.

[5]Richard Rorty, "Putnam and the Relativist Menace," *Journal of Philosophy* 90 (1993): 455, 451-2 (footnotes deleted). Hilary Putnam is a fellow philosopher who shares some but certainly not all of Rorty's philosophical convictions.

[6]There is an important, if technical, difference between true belief that is formed by a person who *generally* exhibits virtue and true belief that is formed through *an act* of virtue. The former is less successful at ruling out cases—called "Gettier counter-examples"—where true beliefs are formed by luck. The latter is much more successful in doing so.

[7]For more on this important question, see Paul K. Moser's forthcoming booklet in this series, *Why Isn't God More Obvious?*

[8]Hugh Ross, *The Fingerprint of God*, 2nd ed. (Orange, Calif.: Promise Publishing, 1991), 121-22.

[9]Michael J. Behe, *Darwin's Black Box* (New York: Touchstone/Simon & Schuster, 1996).

[10]C. S. Lewis, "The Weight of Glory," in *The Weight Of Glory And Other Addresses* (New York: Macmillan, 1949), 1-2.

SUMMARY OF KEY POINTS

The Skeptical Question: "Since we disagree about so many things, do we *really* know what we *think* we know?"

The Skeptical Question in its *modern* form: "Do we *really* know what we *think* we know—especially in religion—when our beliefs are not properly based on evidence?"

The Skeptical Question in its *postmodern* form: "Do we *really* know what we *think* we know since there's no higher viewpoint beyond *your* perspective and *my* perspective?"

Problems with *modern* skepticism:

- The modern skeptic's lofty standard for knowledge rules out many things that should count as knowledge. In fact, it even rules out the modern skeptic's own "standard for knowledge."
- The assumption that science is the best way to knowledge (scientism) depends on an important assumption that is not itself knowable through science.
- Decisions about religious knowledge claims are unavoidable. Practically speaking, in the area of religious faith, "I'm not sure" is equivalent to "No."

The Problem with *postmodern* skepticism:

- The lack of absolute certainty does nothing to undercut knowledge claims. Knowledge of ambiguity is not the same thing as ambiguity about all knowledge claims.
- The postmodern skeptic's critique of truth

must assume the very idea it's critiquing and attempting to revise. The idea of "truth as usefulness," seen as a replacement for the traditional notion of truth, fails to capture our key insights about what it means to say that something "is true."

- The postmodern claims that knowledge is biased and that those who make knowledge claims have ulterior motives are sometimes true. But these facts don't make knowledge impossible. Plus, the postmodern skeptic's attempt to under cut knowledge can itself be seen as an attempt to advance this skeptic's particular agenda.

How we attain knowledge:

- It's important to distinguish between truth and knowledge. Truth is a proper description of the real world. Knowledge is person's grasp of what is true.
- It's impossible to support every belief by following some method. Many particular things are knowable, and people are wise to work at supporting and extending that knowledge.
- Generally, beliefs formed in the course of normal everyday life are reliable. But when a reason to doubt one of those beliefs arises, it's wise to use one of many ways of testing for the truth.
- Knowledge is a belief that corresponds to the real world which is formed through an act of intellectual virtue.

How religious knowledge is possible:

- One should employ standards for knowledge appropriate to the object being known. In the case of God, who isn't some physical object but a divine being, one shouldn't expect the same sort of evidence as one expects for such objects.
- For those who have developed the intellectual virtues and are open to it, the evidence for God is powerful.

Copan, Paul. *"True for You, But Not for Me": Deflating the Slogans That Leave Christians Speechless.* Minneapolis: Bethany, 1998. A response to various objections to Christian belief, especially that of relativism. **Popular level**.

Craig, William Lane. *Reasonable Faith: Christian Truth and Apologetics.* Wheaton, Ill.: Crossway, 1994. A good summary of reasons for thinking that Christianity is true. **Intermediate level**.

DeRose, Keith, and Ted A. Warfield. *Skepticism: A Contemporary Reader.* New York: Oxford University Press, 1999. An excellent collection of essays that represents a range of possible philosophical responses to skepticism. **Advanced level**.

Sire, James W. *Why Should Anyone Believe Anything at All?* Downers Grove, Ill.: InterVarsity Press, 1994. A good response to skepticism and defense of the truth of the Christian faith. Aimed primarily at college students. **Popular level**.

Wood, W. Jay. *Epistemology: Becoming Intellectually Virtuous.* Downers Grove, Ill.: InterVarsity Press, 1998. An excellent introduction to various issues in epistemology (the study of theories of knowledge) from the perspective of the intellectual virtues. **Intermediate level**.

PROJECTED BOOKLETS IN THE RZIM CRITICAL QUESTIONS SERIES

William Craig, *God, Are You There? Five Reasons God Exists and Three Reasons It Makes a Difference* (available)

Paul Copan, *Is Everything Really Relative? Examining the Assumptions of Relativism and the Culture of* Truth *Decay* (available)

David K. Clark and James Beilby, *Why Bother With Truth? Arriving at Knowledge in a Skeptical Society* (available)

Paul K. Moser, *Why Isn't God More Obvious? Finding the God Who Hides and Seeks* (available)

Scott Armstrong, *Who's Shaping My Life? Assessing the Media's Influence on Our Culture*

Darrell Bock, *Can I Trust the Bible? Defending the Bible's Reliability*

Douglas Geivett, *Can a Good God Allow Evil? Making Sense of Suffering*

Klaus Issler, *What Does It Mean To Be Human? Understanding Who We Really Are*

L. T. Jeyachandran *Does the East Have the Answers? Getting Perspective on Eastern Religion and Philosophy*

Mark Linville, *Ethics without God? Defending the Theistic Basis for Morality*

Stuart McAllister, *Born to Shop? Exposing the Threat of a Consumer Culture*

Keith Pavlischek, *Should God Be Excluded from the Public Square? Understanding the Role of Faith in Public Life*

Michael Ramsden, *What's the Point? Finding Meaning and Hope in God*

John Mark Reynolds, *Do the Bible and Science Conflict? Reconciling the Differences*

Ravi Zacharias, *What's So Special About Jesus? Encountering Christ Among the World's Religions*

Paul Chamberlain, *Whose Life Is It Anyway? Assessing Euthanasia and Other Medical-Ethics Issues*

Christopher Wright, *Isn't the God of the Bible Cruel and Vindictive? Understand Ethical Issues in the Bible*

If you have further questions or are in need of additional resources, please contact Ravi Zacharias International Ministries, 4725 Peachtree Corners Circle, Suite 250, Norcross, Georgia 30092.

Order line: 800.448.6766
Fax: 770.729.1729
E-mail: rzim@rzim.com
Website: http://www.gospelcom.net/rzim/

RZIM is a ministry founded by Dr. Ravi Zacharias with the goal to reach and challenge those who shape the ideas of a culture with the credibility of the message of Jesus Christ.

If you are interested in obtaining a first-rate philosophical journal written with articles written by leading Christian philosophers, we encourage you to subscribe to *Philosophia Christi*, the journal of the Evangelical Philosophical Society (EPS). Please contact:

Paul Pardi
35706 25th Pl. South
Federal Way, WA 98003
eps8451@epsociety.org

Published by RZIM
Ravi Zacharias International Ministries
4725 Peachtree Corners Circle, Suite 250
Norcross, Georgia 30092
HYPERLINK http://www.gospelcom.net/rzim/ http://www.gospelcom.net/rzim/

Library of Congress Cataloging-in-Publication Data

2000
Why Bother With Truth? Arriving at Knowledge in a Skeptical Society

ISBN 1-930107-02-1

1. Knowledge, Theory of (Religion).
2. Christianity—Philosophy.